Anastasia
Christmas 1989
with Love
Aunty Debbie +
Uncle Brian xx

Hurdy-Gurdy

This collection of stories and poems, although intended primarily for seven-year-olds, will also please many children of six and eight since children's tastes and abilities vary so widely. I know that some children find it difficult to realise that words on a printed page have originated in someone's imagination, so I have introduced, albeit briefly, all the writers. Maybe the children will discover a writer whose work they particularly enjoy and be encouraged to read more widely. And, although many seven-year-olds will be able readers, I nevertheless hope that parents and teachers will not allow the shared pleasure of reading aloud to become a thing of the past.

Pamela Oldfield

Hurdy-Gurdy

Pamela Oldfield

Illustrated by Linda Birch

Blackie

Contents

For Harriet

First published 1984 by Blackie and Son Limited

British Library Cataloguing in Publication Data
Oldfield, Pamela
Hurdy-gurdy.
I. Title
823'.914[J] PZ7

ISBN 0-216-91644-5

Blackie and Son Limited
Bishopbriggs, Glasgow G64 2NZ
Furnival House, 14/18 High Holborn,
London WC1V 6BX

Printed in Great Britain by Thomson Litho Ltd, East Kilbride, Scotland

The first two stories in this book are by PAMELA OLDFIELD. That's me. I have a son, David, and a daughter, Carole, and when they were much younger, we all enjoyed story times together. I chose all the stories and poems in this anthology, and I do hope you like them. If you would like to write to me about them, I'd be pleased to hear from you.

All the pictures in the book were drawn by a friend of mine called LINDA BIRCH. She lives in a little village near Canterbury and is married with two daughters, Emma and Charlotte. They have been looking forward to seeing Linda's pictures in the finished book.

The Chancellor Who Wouldn't Smile

PAMELA OLDFIELD

Once upon a time there lived a Lord High Chancellor. He lived all by himself (except for his servants) in a large, draughty castle and he never went out and no one ever came in. This was because he was such a bad-tempered, ill-mannered, unreasonable man that no one liked him. Whenever anyone had to speak to him they made it as brief as possible. Even the King didn't like him and never went to the castle, preferring to telephone or write letters.

Now the Lord High Chancellor didn't know he was bad-tempered, ill-mannered and unreasonable and he couldn't understand why he had no friends.

'I live among unfriendly people,' he wrote in his diary. 'I will live and die in this lonely castle and no one will care.' Which is rather sad.

One day a scullery maid came to work in the castle. She was a happy soul, always laughing and singing and she had so many friends she had lost count of them all. Unfortunately she was also a rather clumsy girl and very forgetful. She dropped loud objects like tin trays and buckets and she broke fragile objects like cups and saucers. She was always forgetting what work she had done and doing it again and not doing some work she ought to have done. She was often shouted at for her clumsy and forgetful ways and that made the Lord High Chancellor even more bad-tempered than usual and at last he sent for the cook.

'How can I do my very important work with this noise going on?' he demanded angrily. 'I cannot think straight. Bangings and crashings and shouting and singing! The hall has been scrubbed three times today and my favourite teapot has lost its spout. This castle is becoming a bear garden!' The poor cook didn't know what a bear garden was but the look on the Lord High Chancellor's face frightened her half to death. She promised to speak very severely to the scullery maid, and sent for her right away.

'This castle is becoming a bear garden,' she told the scullery maid. 'You must stop all this noise and think about what you are doing or it will be the sack for you, my girl.'

The scullery maid tried to look very sorry but there was a twinkle in her eye because the cook's cap was crooked and she looked rather funny.

'Now hurry up and finish scrubbing the dining-room,' said the cook. The poor girl burst out laughing because she wasn't scrubbing the dining-room at all. She was scrubbing the hall for the fourth time that day! She laughed and laughed and the cook shouted at her to stop and her cap slipped right down over her eyes. The scullery maid laughed louder than ever.

'That settles it,' roared the cook. 'Out you go, my girl, and don't you show your face here again.'

The poor scullery maid was quite hysterical by this time. Tears of laughter were rolling down her face. When the gardener came in to see what the commotion was all about he thought she was really crying and begged the cook to give her another chance. The cook boxed his ears for his impudence and the scullery maid laughed so much she got a stitch and had to sit down on a handy stool.

Suddenly the Lord High Chancellor appeared in the doorway. He looked more bad-tempered, ill-mannered and unreasonable than ever before in his life. The scullery maid stopped laughing and wiped her eyes on a corner of her apron. The gardener slipped out of the kitchen and hid himself in the potting shed. The cook ran weeping to her bedroom, she was so upset, and the Lord High Chancellor stood glaring down at the scullery maid. She looked a sorry sight in her ragged clothes and he was surprised to find himself feeling sorry for her. After a long silence he gave a little cough and said,

'Er . . . there, there . . . my dear . . .'

He wasn't used to saying nice things to people and he wasn't quite sure how to go about it.

'Um . . . er . . . don't cry now . . . um . . .'

He looked so awkward that the scullery maid was afraid she was going to laugh again and that would never do. She clapped a hand over her mouth and ran past the Lord High Chancellor, down the castle steps and out into the dark wood. She ran and ran and ran.

After she had gone peace descended on the castle. The Lord High Chancellor finished writing an important letter. The cook made an apple pie. The gardener dug over the rosebed. It was very quiet. It was quiet the next day and the day after that. It was quiet for a long time.

The Lord High Chancellor wrote lots of important letters and the King telephoned once or twice – I think twice. The Lord High Chancellor wrote in his diary. 'I live among unfriendly, quiet people. I will live and die here and no one will care . . . and the hall needs a good scrub.'

When he could bear it no longer he sent for the cook.

'Find the scullery maid,' he said, 'and tell her to be my scullery maid again. I miss her laughter and singing. I even miss hearing her dropping things. She must come back.'

Well, they found the scullery maid after a long search but she had gone up in the world. She was no longer a scullery maid but a parlour maid with every other Saturday off. She did not want to go back to scrubbing floors and no one could blame her. So the Lord High Chancellor asked her to marry him. She had to say 'Yes' because he looked so awkward when he said nice things to people, and they were married the very next week.

Now if you think that being married to a happy wife changed the Lord High Chancellor you are wrong. He was still bad-tempered, ill-mannered and unreasonable – but in a happy sort of way!

Buster's Day Out

PAMELA OLDFIELD

'Buster is going to love the beach,' said Debbie happily. 'He can swim in the sea – '

'And play with the ball,' said Bet who carried an old tennis ball for the purpose.

'I expect he'll find another dog to play with,' said Steve.

'He sure is going to have fun,' said Howie, and Buster, knowing that they were talking about him, ran round them in circles, barking his delight.

The Gumby Gang were on their way to the beach for a swim.

They had all said 'parsnips' – even Bet – and they were now hoping for fun and adventure. They took it in turns to carry the old haversack which contained the sandwiches and a flask of coffee plus a bottle of water and a bone for Buster. The sun was shining and the lane was full of eager children heading towards the beach with buckets and spades.

'The first thing I shall do,' said Steve, 'is to run along the breakwater and dive in.'

'All your clothes will get wet,' said Bet.

'I shall take them off first,' said Steve.

'But you said the first thing you'd do – '

'Don't argue, Bet,' said Debbie hastily. 'You

know what Steve means. You're just being awkward.'

'I wish I had an aqualung,' said Howie. 'I'd swim around looking at all the tropical fish.'

'Tropical fish?' said Steve. 'In Winchingsea? You'll be lucky to see a crab. The water's always sandy and you can't see a thing . . . I wonder what Gran put in the sandwiches?'

'Cheese and pickle,' said Debbie, 'and egg and lettuce. I know because I helped her make them.'

'Ugh!' said Steve. 'I don't fancy them!'

'Don't eat them then,' said Debbie. 'All the more for the rest of us. Maybe Buster will let you share his bone.'

Squabbling happily, they reached the beach, and found a space. In no time they were in their swimsuits and rushing into the water. As Steve had warned, it was fairly rough and milky brown with sand. Debbie began to screech as soon as it lapped her ankles.

'Oh, it's freezing! It's awful. I can't even feel my feet. They must be blue with cold!'

'Save you wearing socks,' said Steve.

He splashed past her and, plunging underneath the water, came up gasping for air and shivering. 'It's O.K. when you get used to it,' he said.

Bet paddled around in the shallow water and Howie sat down in it, shrieking horribly that it

Teas

was too cold. It was all too much for poor Buster who had never in his life seen so much water or so many people. He was amazed to see the children submerging themselves in the water. Convinced that they were in terrible danger, he began to bark.

'Quit that barking, Buster,' cried Howie. 'We're O.K. We aren't drowning or anything.'

But Buster was still not happy and tried desperately to reach them. He ran forward every time the waves receded and leaped back nervously when they turned again. And all the time he barked furiously until heads began to turn and people began to grumble.

'Can't you keep your dog quiet?' demanded a young man in glasses. 'It's deafening.'

Debbie went rather pink. 'I'll try,' she said. Scrambling out of the water she was met by Buster who barked a greeting which was even noisier than before.

'Ssh! Silly boy,' she said. 'Why can't you behave like all the other dogs? They're not making such an exhibition. Now sit!'

Buster put his head on one side as though she had gone suddenly crazy.

'I mean it,' she said sternly. 'Sit! That's better. And don't move.' He sat subdued as she marched back into the water, then he dropped down miserably on the sand.

'Wow!' said Howie admiringly. 'You sure fixed him.'

'It's nothing,' said Debbie. 'He just needs a firm hand.'

After that Buster was quiet . . . very quiet!

'He's too quiet,' said Steve ten minutes later. 'Go and have a look, Bet, and see what he's doing.'

'He's probably asleep,' said Debbie and they watched as Bet trotted up the beach to investigate. When she reached the dog she gave a squeal of horror.

'He's eaten the sandwiches!' she cried. 'Oh, Buster, you bad, awful dog!'

Debbie, Steve and Howie ran up on to the sand and they all glared at Buster who was swallowing the last crust.

'Well,' said Steve. 'All I can say is thank goodness he doesn't like coffee!'

They looked at each other and the idea of Buster unscrewing the thermos flask set them all laughing.

'Let's not grumble at him,' said Howie. 'He sure is awful but he's only a dog. Dogs have very small brains.'

'His must be the size of a pea!' said Steve. 'But we'll give him another chance. Let's have a cup of coffee to warm ourselves up.'

They sat down and Debbie poured a generous helping into the beaker and they drank a few mouthfuls. Then she screwed the top on again.

'I've got an idea,' said Steve. 'Maybe if Buster could swim with us he'd understand that we're not in danger. I vote we carry him into the water, then let him swim.'

The others agreed and Steve and Howie staggered into the water carrying Buster between them, much to the amusement of everyone else on the beach. When the water reached their knees, they lowered Buster gently into it.

'Good boy,' said Debbie. 'Isn't the water lovely?'

Buster didn't think so. He gave her a baleful look and set off, swimming frantically towards the beach.

'No!' cried Bet. 'Come back, Buster. You'll like it.'

But, ignoring her, the dog trotted out onto the sand and shook himself, spraying water all over an elderly couple who were sitting in their deckchairs, minding their own business.

'Oh no!' groaned Steve. 'I can't bear it.'

The elderly gentleman jumped to his feet and waved his arms at Buster to 'shoo' him away. Poor Buster was so surprised he sprang backwards and landed right in the middle of someone's picnic. His back leg went straight into a large meat pie and his tail spilled a jug of lemonade into someone's lap. There was pandemonium!

'My beautiful meat pie!'

'Get away, you horrible brute!'

'Get out of it!'

'Help!'

The Gumby Gang dared not look. It was so awful. Buster, frightened by all the noise, raced off in the opposite direction, straight into a well-behaved Alsatian who was watching the drama with polite interest. There was a short, sharp scuffle.

'Quick!' cried Debbie. 'We must rescue Buster or he'll be eaten alive. That dog's much bigger than him.'

The children rushed out of the water. Piercing howls, screams and a fierce snapping filled the air as the two dogs whirled around the beach, scattering holidaymakers in all directions. Before the children could reach him, Buster broke free, streaked away along the beach and disappeared.

'He sure is travelling!' said Howie, impressed.

'He's doing ninety miles an hour at least,' said Debbie.

Bet burst into tears, declaring that they had lost Buster forever.

'Of course we haven't,' said Debbie, not feeling too sure about it. 'We must go after him.'

It was a good time to go. Angry people were descending upon them in dozens so they hastily packed up their belongings and set off running along the beach to find Buster.

They didn't find him. An hour later they gave up searching and went home to tell Steve's Gran the dreadful news.

'Buster?' she said, surprised. 'Oh, he came home ages ago. He ran under the bed and wouldn't come out so I left him there.'

They rushed upstairs and hauled Buster out from his hiding place. Then they stared at him in dismay. In his mouth he held a sandal which he had found on his travels along the beach.

'It's all chewed up,' said Bet. 'Ooh, you bad dog!'

Buster hurriedly returned to the shelter of the bed and the Gumby Gang went downstairs, thoughtfully.

'Let's not go on the beach tomorrow,' said Steve and for once they were all agreed.

* * *

WALTER DE LA MARE was born in 1873 and died in 1956. He wrote plays and stories as well as poems, and he liked writing for children. The two poems I have chosen come from a book called *Peacock Pie*. Many of Walter de la Mare's poems have a great feeling of mystery about them like 'The Ride-By-Nights'. Others are about nature, childhood and dreams.

The Ride-By-Nights

WALTER DE LA MARE

Up on their brooms the Witches stream,
Crooked and black in the crescent's gleam;
One foot high, and one foot low,
Bearded, cloaked, and cowled, they go,
'Neath Charlie's Wain they twitter and tweet,
And away they swarm 'neath the Dragon's feet,
With a whoop and a flutter they swing and sway,
And surge pell-mell down the Milky Way.
Betwixt the legs of the glittering Chair
They hover and squeak in the empty air.
Then round they swoop past the glimmering Lion
To where Sirius barks behind huge Orion;
Up, then, and over to wheel amain,
Under the silver, and home again.

Chicken

WALTER DE LA MARE

Clapping her platter stood plump Bess,
And all across the green
Came scampering in, on wing and claw,
Chicken fat and lean: –
Dorking, Spaniard, Cochin China,
Bantams sleek and small,
Like feathers blown in a great wind,
They came at Bessie's call.

ALISON UTTLEY died some years ago, but when she was a girl she lived with her family on a farm on a hilltop in Derbyshire. She loved the countryside and many of her stories are about flowers, birds, insects or animals.

The Wind In A Frolic

ALISON UTTLEY

One day the Wind awoke from a little nap under the quiet trees. He stretched himself lazily, and yawned with wide-open mouth, so that the bees and butterflies resting on the flowers were blown away by a tiny gust.

'Oh! Ho-o-o!' he yawned, again. 'I'll go for a stroll, and say how-do-ye-do to the village folk. I'm sure they've missed me lately. I'll go and cheer them up, play with them, amuse them. Yes, that's what I'll do today.'

He picked up his long length from the mossy ground, and stalked off down the path, snapping twigs from the trees with his slender fingers, blowing the leaves with his breath.

Now he hadn't gone far when he met a little boy going to school. Such a neat little, nice little, clean little boy, with his cap on his head, and his school-bag on his back!

'How d'ye do?' said the wind, and he put out one thin finger, twitched the cap and flung it up in a sycamore-tree. There it hung till the nice little boy climbed up and got it down, but his hands were dirty, and his hair awry. The Wind sat on the ground watching, waiting for the little boy to laugh.

'Bother the wind!' exclaimed the little boy, and he stuffed his cap in his pocket and went whistling to school.

'That was clever of me,' said the Wind, 'But he wasn't amused. I must do something better next time.'

He went a bit farther, and overtook a little girl. A few drops of rain were falling by this time, and she put up her umbrella.

'I always think umbrellas are such comical things,' said the Wind, 'don't you?'

The little girl answered never a word, but held tight to the handle when she felt the Wind's presence.

'There it goes!' cried the Wind, putting his face under it, and giving a small puff. Away it went, inside out, and the Wind laughed and laughed at the funny sight. But the little girl didn't laugh. She ran after her umbrella, and picked it up sadly. It was her birthday umbrella the Wind had spoilt, but of course the Wind didn't know that.

'Dear-a-me,' said the Wind. 'I thought that

was amusing. I must find someone else to tease.'

He went rollicking along the road, and the cows and horses turned their backs or stood close to the hedges for shelter. Then he saw a farm man carrying hay on his back. The Wind blew and blew, till the man staggered against a wall and the hay went floating off in the air.

The Wind laughed to see the sight, but the man grumbled and groaned as he collected it together again, and tied it with a rope.

'The wind's something awful!' said he crossly, and the Wind, very much surprised, skipped away to find someone with a sense of humour.

Along came a woman with a basket of eggs, and the Wind hurried up to her.

'Madam,' said he politely, taking off his pointed hat. 'Madam, may I carry your basket for you?' He put a hand on the basket, but the woman felt the strong gale around her, and held on with all her might. What was happening to the weather, for the wind to blow like that all of a sudden? she wondered. Her skirts flew out behind her, her hat blew off, but she wouldn't let the basket go. Then the wind tossed an egg in the air, and it fell with a splash of yellow.

'Isn't that a joke! Ha! Ha! If only you would give me your basket, I would show you even funnier things. Eggs sailing in the air, and dropping like raindrops!'

'Goodness!' cried the woman. 'There's one of my eggs! Two pence gone. This wind's a regular nuisance.'

She held the basket close to her side to protect it, but the Wind had flown away to find someone else.

He blew the hens in the farmyard, so that they ran squawking to the barn, and he drove the dog to the kennel. He shook the sign outside the village inn, and rattled the shutters on the wall. He threw a slate off the roof, and dropped a chimney pot. The Wind chuckled at all these pranks, but the people frowned and shut their doors.

Then away went the Wind, away, away, over the fields and woods. He felt very unhappy, for nobody laughed, nobody wanted the Wind's frolic. He felt so dejected that he began to walk, and then to crawl, with his head bent, and his arms hanging limp.

'There isn't a laugh left in the world! It's a sad, sad place, and I shall go away and play with the Polar bears and penguins. They will welcome me.'

He didn't really want to go to such cold places, and he glanced round to see if there was still a chance of a laugh.

On top of the hill was a windmill, with great sails lying idle. In the orchard nearby was a clothes-line full of washing, and a little boy ran up and down, trying to fly a kite.

The Wind tripped lightly to the house, and blew, just a little. The clothes flapped and sank again. He blew harder, and the clothes began to dance. Sheets cracked with a delicious sound, pyjamas seemed to have invisible legs, coats and petticoats were full of fat windy people who swung up and down on the line. The little boy's kite flew up in the air, and soared on the end of the string like a blue bird. The great sails of the windmill with many a creak and groan began to turn, and then went rapidly round and round.

The miller and his wife came running to the door.

'Here's the wind at last,' said they, laughing to one another. 'It will grind my corn,' said the miller, joyfully.

'It will dry my washing,' said his wife, as she watched the clothes swing in the wind.

'Look at my kite!' said the little boy. 'Isn't it going well! Like an eagle! I do like this wind,' and he ran round and round with the Wind tugging at the little blue kite.

'Thank goodness, I've found people who like me! I shall often come and see this laughing family. The world's not so bad after all,' said the Wind, and he danced round and round the windmill, puffing out his cheeks, and whistling a merry tune.

The Rainbow

ALISON UTTLEY

Tom Oliver had been fishing all the morning in the little brook which ran down the fields – the silver shining brook which rattled over the stones, grinding them into pebbles, the stream which seized the meadow grasses and dragged them by their green hair, so that they looked like water-nymphs, swimming in the rapid little torrent. Tadpoles and minnows and Jack Sharps were the only creatures that lived there, for the brook was so noisy that the big fish preferred to swim in the quiet river lower down the valley. Tom's mother would not allow him to go near the deep pools and hollows of that tranquil water, but when he leaned over the humpbacked bridge, with his face half-buried in the ferns on the edge, he could watch the dark slim shapes mysteriously moving down below, and sometimes he saw a real fisherman in waders standing in the water, and landing a speckled trout.

But the brook was a splendid place for a boy's fishing. The quickest way to catch anything was to dangle an empty jampot in the water, or to dip a brown hand under a stone, although Tom preferred to do it properly, and to use a fishing rod made of a hazel switch, with a bit of string on the end, and almost anything for bait – a holly berry, a cherry, an acorn.

He was fishing like this, sitting cross-legged on a stone under an alder-tree, and the sun was shining brightly, so that speckles and sparkles of light flashed about on the water, and flickering nets of sunshine lay on the bottom of the brook. Suddenly he felt a bite, and the cherry bobbed and dipped as if something very much alive was on the end.

Quickly he pulled in his line, and there, wriggling on the end, was no minnow, or Jack Sharp, or Miller's thumb, but a rainbow, a curving iridescent rainbow, with all the seven lovely colours in its arching back. It leaped and danced on its tail so that Tom had much to do to catch it.

It was quite a little rainbow when Tom carried it home, all writhing and slipping in his fingers, but when he put it in the garden, it grew so large that it stretched across from the lilac bush to the silver birch-tree, in a beautiful curving sweep of misty colours. He could no longer hold it, for it slithered through his hands like dew-drops, but there it hung, in a fine archway, a marvel for all the world to see.

Tom's mother left her wash-tub, and stood at the kitchen door for a moment.

'Yes, it's a rainbow, right enough,' said she. 'I've never seen a rainbow in our garden before. It cheers one up to see it,' and she went back to her work. Tom spent all day looking at his rainbow, running his fingers through its elusive colour bands, catching the blue and orange in his hands. The chaffinches fluttered through it, and the tom tits swung on the top, as if it were a bough of a celestial tree, so that their wings were flecked with many lights.

A blackbird whistled at the foot where the arch rested on the lilac-tree, and a thrush sang at the other end, on the silver birch. All the birds saw the rainbow hanging in the garden, and they called to one another to play in and out of the great arch.

'It would make a nice clothes' line,' said Tom's mother, thoughtfully, and she carried out the washing-basket and started to peg the shirts and towels on the bands of colour. But they slipped through and fell to the ground, and the rainbow shook itself so that drops of water sprinkled them like rain. With a sigh Mrs Oliver gathered them up and took them to the drying-ground. It was a pity she could not make use of such a nice clean rope of colour, for it was a pretty sight.

The curious thing about it was that some other people could not see it. Cross Mr Jenkins, the chimney-sweep next door, saw nothing at all. Mrs Stone, who kept the little grocery store in her front window, saw nothing either, although she put on her spectacles and peered quite close, but little Jemima Stone could see it, and she came into the garden and stood with Tom Oliver, watching the rainbow's twinkling colours, which changed as the children moved.

Night came, but still the rainbow glowed in the garden. Tom's mother said it would disappear when the sun set, and certainly even Tom's sharp eyes couldn't see it in the dark, but when he moved his fingers across it he could feel it like a ripple in the air, and he knew it was there.

The stars came out, and the moon rose above the hill. Tom leaned from his bedroom window, and looked down to the garden. Yes, the bow was still there, with strange pale colours of silver, and on the highest point of the arch a nightingale perched itself and sang its haunting passionate song. That was indeed a sight to remember!

The next morning when Tom sprang from bed and poked his head out of the casement the first thing he saw was the rainbow, all fresh and bright, swinging lightly across the garden. So it hadn't gone! Surely somebody would see it to-day! He wanted to share the good news with all the village.

He ran off to school with his bag flapping on his back, eager to tell his friends about it.

'We've got a rainbow in our back garden,' he boasted.

'Don't believe you,' said one.

'Rainbows don't belong to gardens,' said another.

'You come home with me, and I'll show you,' said Tom.

When the boys followed him through the garden gate they said there was nothing there, and mocked at Tom.

'It's hanging in the lilac-tree. Can't you see it? You must all be blind,' said Tom, exasperated, and he put his head on one side and pointed out the lovely colours spanning the trees in the airy filmy archway.

'Oh leave him! It's all nonsense! There's no rainbow! Leave him to his moonshine,' they exclaimed, and off they ran to look for birds' nests in the hedges.

Tom hung his head and walked into the house. Only his mother and little Jemima Stone could see the rainbow. What was the good of it if nobody believed in it? Perhaps it wasn't there at all, and he had imagined it. He ran to the door and looked out, and was just in time to see the rainbow rapidly growing smaller. It curled into a little ball and fell in a wreath of colour to the ground.

Although he hunted and hunted he couldn't find it. He searched among the cabbages, the carrots, and onions, but there was no rainbow. He looked among the pansies, the sweet-williams and bachelor's buttons, but there was no sign of a rainbow among the flowers. Where could it have gone? He turned sadly away, unhappy that he had doubted and so lost his treasure, when a sparkle on the rubbish heap caught his eye. He picked up a little prism of glass, and held it to the sun. Bands of coloured light fell from it, and he shouted with joy.

'I've caught the rainbow again, Mother. It's shut up in this glass, like a ship in a bottle!'

He turned it this way and that and let the spectrum of colour fall on his hands.

'Where was it, Tom?' asked Mrs Oliver, running to the door.

'On the rubbish heap. Look at it, all the colours, and not one missing. Violet, indigo, blue, green, yellow, orange, red. All of them, fast in the glass.'

'It can't escape me this time,' he continued, twirling the prism. 'I can take it to school, and the boys must believe me.'

He put the prism from the chandelier in his pocket and ran laughing down the lane, and when he showed it to the other boys they all agreed they could see the rainbow now.

But his mother returned to her wash-tub, and bent over the clothes. There, dancing over the soap-suds, glimmering in the bubbles, were a thousand little rainbows of light.

'I've got a bit of that rainbow, too,' she told herself. 'Once I thought it lived in the sky, and now I've seen it even in my old wash-tub. Who would believe it?'

She took up her soap and rubbed the clothes, and then she began to sing with happiness.

* * *

I found the next poem in a book called *Salt-Sea Verse*. It is by CHRISTINA ROSSETTI who, as you can guess by her name, had an Italian father. She also had a famous brother, Dante Gabriel Rossetti, who was a painter. What a talented family! Christina Rossetti died nearly a hundred years ago but her poems will never be forgotten.

What Are Heavy? Sea-Sand And Sorrow

CHRISTINA ROSSETTI

What are heavy? sea-sand and sorrow:
What are brief? today and tomorrow:
What are frail? Spring blossoms and youth:
What are deep? the ocean and truth.

Another poem from *Salt-Sea Verse* is called 'The Fishermen's Song' and is anonymous. That means we don't know who wrote it. Possibly it never was a poem but a song which the fishermen sang as they hauled in the fish or sat on the beach mending their nets.

The Fishermen's Song

ANONYMOUS

O blithely shines the bonny sun
Upon the Isle of May,
And blithely rolls the morning tide
Into St Andrew's bay.

When haddocks leave the Firth of Forth,
And mussels leave the shore,
When oysters climb up Berwick Law,
We'll go to sea no more,
No more,
We'll go to sea no more.

* * *

When I was a child my parents used to read aloud stories written by a man called A. A. MILNE (his first names were Alan Alexander). The stories are all about his son Christopher Robin and his toys, and they are still my favourites today. He wrote a lot of poems, too, like this one which comes from a book called *When We Were Very Young*.

Bad Sir Brian Botany

A. A. MILNE

Sir Brian had a battleaxe with great big knobs
on;
He went among the villagers and blipped them
on the head.
On Wednesday and on Saturday, but mostly on
the latter day,
He called at all the cottages, and this is what he
said:

'I am Sir Brian!' *(ting-ling)*
'I am Sir Brian!' *(rat-tat)*
'I am Sir Brian, as bold as a lion—
Take *that!* – and *that!* – and *that!'*

Sir Brian had a pair of boots with great big spurs on,
A fighting pair of which he was particularly fond.
On Tuesday and Friday, just to make the street look tidy,
He'd collect the passing villagers and kick them in the pond.

'I am Sir Brian!' *(sper-lash!)*
'I am Sir Brian!' *(sper-losh!)*
'I am Sir Brian, as bold as a lion—
Is anyone else for a wash?'

Sir Brian awoke one morning, and he couldn't find his battleaxe;
He walked into the village in his second pair of boots.
He had gone a hundred paces, when the street was full of faces,
And the villagers were round him with ironical salutes.

'You are Sir Brian? Indeed!
You are Sir Brian? Dear, dear!
You are Sir Brian, as bold as a lion?
Delighted to meet you here!'

Sir Brian went a journey, and he found a lot of duckweed:

They pulled him out and dried him, and they
blipped him on the head.
They took him by the breeches, and they hurled
him into ditches,
And they pushed him under waterfalls, and this
is what they said:

'You are Sir Brian – don't laugh,
You are Sir Brian – don't cry;
You are Sir Brian, as bold as a lion—
Sir Brian, the lion, good-bye!'

Sir Brian struggled home again, and chopped up
his battleaxe,
Sir Brian took his fighting boots, and threw
them in the fire.
He is quite a different person now he hasn't got
his spurs on,
And he goes about the village as B. Botany,
Esquire.

'I am Sir Brian? Oh, *no*!
I am Sir Brian? Who's he?
I haven't got any title, I'm Botany—
Plain Mr Botany (B).'

* * *

Did you know that you can dial a number on the telephone and hear a three-minute bedtime story? H. E. TODD is very well known for his stories about Bobby and Barbara Brewster, but he has also written some telephone stories and I have chosen these two from the *Dial-a-Story Book*. H. E. Todd also goes into schools to read his stories. Perhaps you've been lucky enough to see him.

A Puffin Called Percy

H. E. TODD

Last year, the Brewsters spent their holiday in their caravan at a lovely spot near the sea in Cornwall.

On the sands one day, they saw a young puffin, with a pink beak and a serious expression on his face, standing alone and bewildered. His parents had flown away leaving him to look after himself, which is what mother and father puffins really do when they are tired of catching fish for their young and think it is time for them to look after themselves.

'Poor little thing,' said Mrs Brewster. 'We must take him back to our caravan.'

So she picked him up and Barbara and Bobby gently stroked his head.

He soon became a part of the family, and they gave him a name, Percy the puffin. He joined in all the fun and sometimes even tried to help with the washing-up by jumping in the sink.

Of course, life was easy for him. All he had to do was to waddle about while people caught fish for him, which saved him a lot of trouble. By the end of the holidays he was bigger and stronger.

On the last day, the Brcwsters had no heart to leave him behind, so they decided to take him home with them. He looked serious all the time, but he seemed to enjoy the journey.

At home, he was still part of the family and made great friends with all their friends. As he grew, he ate more and more fish. The fish-monger thought that the Brewsters must be living on fish until they explained that they needed it for a puffin.

But after a time the local cats started to take an interest in Percy, and the Brewsters did not like the expression on some of the cats' faces. They looked far too hungry! In the end it became clear that it was no longer safe for Percy to go on living with them.

So they wrote to the zoo and asked whether they could take in a puffin. The zoo people replied with the name and address of a man living in Cornwall who was often willing to look after lost birds, and when the Brewsters

wrote to him he replied, 'Yes': they could send Percy to him.

One sad evening they drove Percy to Paddington station, and on the way he stood at the back window of the car for his last sight of London. At the station they packed him in a strong cardboard box, with holes punched in the side to allow him to breathe, and then handed him over to the guard of the midnight Cornish express. The guard promised to feed Percy regularly with fish and keep his box the right way up. It would never have done for him to travel all the way to Cornwall on his head, would it?

In the guard's van, they took a last look at Percy through the holes of his box, and he must have guessed he was leaving them, for Barbara and Bobby thought they saw for the very first time a brave smile on his pink-beaked face.

As the train drew away they all walked back along the platform with tears in their eyes – and the largest tears were in the eyes of Bobby and Barbara Brewster.

But there was no need to feel sad for long. After a time a letter came from the man in Cornwall telling them that Percy the puffin had spent a few days in the bird sanctuary and then one day waddled by himself down to the sea-shore and fluttered happily away.

So now, there he is, waddling and fluttering by the sea which, after all, is a far better home for a puffin than a caravan or a house in a town.

And he is now clever enough to catch his own fish, which are far fresher than the fish they bought him from the fishmongers.

Penny For The Guy

H. E. TODD

Last October the children of Mr Limcano's class built a Guy for Guy Fawkes day. They took a lot of trouble. He had the correct costume, and Barbara and Bobby Brewster made him a papier-mâché face that looked exactly like the pictures of Guy Fawkes in the history books. The Headmistress was so delighted that she invited the parents to come and see him on the evening of 4th November. The parents and other children were so impressed that they dropped lots of pennies in his box, and the total came to £5.75 and three trouser buttons!

On the morning of 5th November, Barbara asked Mr Limcano in class, 'Please, sir, have you one of your magic words in your notebook for Guy Fawkes?'

'I will see,' said Mr Limcano, and after he had consulted his magic notebook under the letter G, he looked straight at the Guy and said, 'Gilli-gilli-gay-guy Fee-fie-fawkes.'

There was a flash, and the Guy sat up and shouted, 'Down with King James.' And then, before they could stop him, he shot off in his trolley, straight out of the door, through the playground, and out of the school gates, yelling 'BLOW UP THE HOUSES OF PARLIAMENT!'

They ran after him but could not catch him up. Then Constable Wilkins rode by on his bicycle.

Later that afternoon, Constable Wilkins rang up the school and told the Headmistress, 'I am glad to report, madam, that the man who claims to be Guy Fawkes is being held at the police station, and will appear in the Magistrates' Court tomorrow morning. Please ask Mr Limcano to appear as a witness at 10 a.m.'

On the following morning, Mr Limcano attended the court. The magistrate was a stern man with a beard.

'What is your name?' he asked the prisoner.

'Guy Fawkes,' said the man.

'If you do not behave yourself, my man, I shall commit you for contempt of court,' said the magistrate. 'Constable Wilkins, please make your report.' Constable Wilkins cleared his throat in an important manner. 'On the morning of Tuesday 5th November, I was proceeding along the High Street,' he said, 'when I saw a man in a cart shouting, "BLOW UP THE HOUSES OF PARLIAMENT!"'

'There's no need for *you* to shout, Constable,' said the magistrate. Then he turned to the Guy.

'What have you to say to that, sir?' he asked.

'BLOW THEM TO SMITHEREENS!' yelled the Guy.

'Any more of your impudence and you will

go straight to prison,' said the magistrate. Then he asked, 'Is anything known of this man?'

'Yes, sir,' said Mr Limcano.

'What have you to say then?' asked the magistrate.

Mr Limcano looked straight at the Guy and said, 'Gilli-gilli-gay-guy Fee-fie-fawkes.'

'Any more of that, sir, and I shall commit you to prison as well,' said the magistrate. But he never did, because the Guy in the box slumped down in his seat and collapsed.

'Fetch a glass of water,' cried the magistrate. It did no good, because by saying the magic words Mr Limcano had turned the Guy back into a sack filled with straw with a papier-mâché face!

That is nearly the end of the story, but not quite.

When the case was over Mr Limcano had to push the Guy back to school in his push-cart through the streets. The people who saw him were so impressed that they insisted on dropping coins into the box, and by the time Mr Limcano had reached the school he had collected £11.25 and five trouser buttons!

* * *

Do you like poems that make you laugh? If you do you'll be pleased to know that MAX FATCHEN has written a book full of funny poems. It's called *Songs For My Dog and Other People* and the next three poems are from that book. Max also writes stories for children and he is very well known in Australia where he lives.

Catnap

MAX FATCHEN

My cat sleeps
with her claws
clasped
and her long tail
curled.

My cat twitches
her tabby cheek
for the mice
that squeak
and the milk that
flows
by her pink, pink nose
in the purring warmth
of my cat's world.

Oh Erica, Not Again!

MAX FATCHEN

Every time we go on the pier,
Or down to the sea, that is,
Erica says she is feeling queer
And it makes her poor head whizz.

Erica says she likes the land,
And there isn't, alas, much doubt,
As soon as she steps on a trippers' boat
Erica's legs give out.

Erica's hands will clutch the rail.
She hears the timbers creak.
She wonders where the lifebelts are –
Or if we've sprung a leak.

There's never a sign of storm or gale
But Mother's crying 'Quick!'
And so it's just the same old tale,
Erica's sick!

Who's Scared Now?

MAX FATCHEN

I'm warning you.
Don't scare me.
Don't go 'Boo'.
Will you?
Don't say you're from space
Or some awful place.
That you're a deep-sea creature
Or a late-night movie monster,
Will you?
Because –
ZAP!
POW!
I'm disintegrating you now.
Click,
Tick!
You are reassembled
And changed,
Your matter
Rearranged,

Thirteen million light years away,
If it's a day,
On the planet Zen,
With a scratchy pen,
Doing four million lines,
In the Homework Mines.
And it serves you right
For frightening me last night.

Two brothers called JACOB and WILHELM GRIMM lived a long time ago in the country of Germany. At that time there were many folk tales and fairy stories that had never been written down. The two brothers decided to discover as many as they could in case the stories were ever forgotten. They became famous for their collection of fairy tales which contains this one about three strange musicians.

The Travelling Musicians

THE BROTHERS GRIMM

An honest farmer had once an ass, that had been a faithful servant to him a great many years, but was now growing old and every day more and more unfit for work. His master therefore was tired of keeping him and began to think of putting an end to him; but the ass, who saw that some mischief was in the wind, took himself slyly off, and began his journey towards the great city. 'For there,' he thought, 'I may turn musician.'

After he had travelled a little way, he spied a dog lying by the road-side and panting as if he were very tired. 'What makes you pant so, my friend?' said the ass. 'Alas!' said the dog, 'my master was going to knock me on the head, because I am old and weak, and can no longer make myself useful to him in hunting, so I ran away; but what can I do to earn my livelihood?'

'Hark ye!' said the ass, 'I am going to the great city to turn musician; suppose you go with me, and try what you can do in the same way?'

The dog said he was willing, and they jogged on together.

They had not gone far before they saw a cat sitting in the middle of the road and making a most rueful face.

'Pray, my good lady,' said the ass, 'what's the matter with you? You look quite out of spirits!'

'Ah me!' said the cat, 'how can one be in good spirits when one's life is in danger? Because I am beginning to grow old, and had rather lie at my ease by the fire than run about the house after mice, my mistress laid hold of me, and was going to drown me; and though I have been lucky enough to get away from her, I do not know what I am to live upon.'

'O!' said the ass, 'by all means go with us to the great city; you are a good night singer, and may make your fortune as a musician.'

The cat was pleased with the thought, and joined the party.

Soon afterwards, as they were passing by a farmyard, they saw a cock perched upon a gate, and screaming out with all his might and main.

'Bravo!' said the ass, 'upon my word you make a famous noise; pray what is all this about?'

'Why,' said the cock, 'I was just now saying that we should have fine weather for our washing-day, and yet my mistress and the cook don't thank me for my pains, but threaten to cut off my head tomorrow, and make broth of me for the guests that are coming on Sunday!'

'Heaven forbid!' said the ass. 'Come with us, Master Chanticleer; it will be better, at any rate, than staying here to have your head cut off! Besides, who knows? If we take care to sing in tune, we may get up some kind of concert; so come along with us.'

'With all my heart,' said the cock; so they all four went on jollily together. They could not, however, reach the great city the first day; so when night came on, they went into a wood to sleep. The ass and the dog laid themselves down under a great tree, and the cat climbed up into the branches; while the cock, thinking that the higher he sat the safer he should be, flew up to the very top of the tree, and then, according to his custom, before he went to sleep, looked out on all sides of him to see that everything was well. In doing this, he saw afar off something bright and shining; and calling to his companions said:

'There must be a house no great way off, for I see a light.'

'If that be the case,' said the ass, 'we had better change our quarters, for our lodging is not the best in the world!'

'Besides,' added the dog, 'I should not be the worse for a bone or two, or a bit of meat.'

So they walked off together towards the spot where Chanticleer had seen the light; and as they drew near, it became larger and brighter, till they at last came close to a house in which a gang of robbers lived.

The ass, being the tallest of the company, marched up to the windows and peeped in.

'Well, Donkey,' said Chanticleer, 'what do you see?'

'What do I see?' replied the ass. 'Why, I see a table spread with all kinds of good things, and robbers sitting round it making merry.'

'That would be a noble lodging for us,' said the cock.

'Yes,' said the ass, 'if we could only get in.'

So they consulted together how they should contrive to get the robbers out; and at last they hit upon a plan. The ass placed himself upright on his hind-legs, with his fore-feet resting against the window; the dog got upon his back; the cat scrambled up to the dog's shoulders, and the cock flew up and sat upon the cat's head. When all was ready, a signal was given, and they began their music. The ass brayed, the dog barked, the cat mewed, and the cock screamed;

and then they all broke through the window at once, and came tumbling into the room amongst the broken glass, with a most hideous clatter! The robbers, who had been not a little frightened by the opening concert, had now no doubt that some frightful hobgoblin had broken in upon them, and scampered away as fast as they could.

The coast once clear, our travellers soon sat down, and dispatched what the robbers had left, with as much eagerness as if they had not expected to eat again for a month. As soon as they had satisfied themselves, they put out the lights, and each once more sought out a resting-place to his own liking. The donkey laid himself down upon a heap of straw in the yard; the dog stretched upon a mat behind the door; the cat rolled herself up on the hearth before the warm ashes; and the cock perched upon a beam on top of the house; and, as they were all rather tired with their journey, they soon fell asleep.

But about midnight, when the robbers saw from afar that the lights were out and that all seemed quiet, they began to think that they had been in too great a hurry to run away; and one of them, who was bolder than the rest, went to see what was going on. Finding everything still, he marched into the kitchen, and groped about until he found a match in order to light a candle; and then, espying the glittering fiery eyes of the cat, he mistook them for live coals, and held the match to them to light it. But the cat, not understanding this joke, sprung at his face, and spat, and scratched at him. This frightened him dreadfully, and away he ran to the back door; but there the dog jumped up and bit him in the leg, and as he was crossing over the yard the ass

kicked him; and the cock, who had been awakened by the noise, crowed with all his might. At this, the robber ran back as fast as he could to his comrades, and told the captain how a horrid witch had got into the house, and had spat at him and scratched his face with her long bony fingers; how a man with a knife in his hand had hidden himself behind the door, and stabbed him in the leg; how a black monster stood in the yard and struck him with a club, and how the devil sat upon the top of the house and cried out, 'Throw the rascal up here!'

After this the robbers never dared to go back to the house: but the musicians were so pleased with their quarters, that they took up their abode there; and there they are, I dare say, at this very day.

* * *

KIT WRIGHT is a very tall man and some people call him the tallest poet in England! Kit was once a teacher but now he spends his time writing and reading his poems to children. You may have seen him on the television.

Babbling And Gabbling

KIT WRIGHT

My Granny's an absolute corker,
My Granny's an absolute cracker,

But she's Britain's speediest talker
And champion yackety-yacker!

Everyone's fond of my Granny,
Everyone thinks she's nice,
But before you can say Jack Robinson,
My Granny's said it twice!

It's Winter, It's Winter

KIT WRIGHT

It's winter, it's winter, it's wonderful winter,
When everyone lounges around in the sun!

It's winter, it's winter, it's wonderful winter,
When everyone's brown like a steak
overdone!

It's winter, it's winter, it's wonderful winter,
It's swimming and surfing and hunting for
conkers!

It's winter, it's winter, it's wonderful winter,
And I am completely and utterly bonkers!

* * *

CATHERINE STORR used to be a doctor, but then she decided to become a full-time writer. One of her stories called *Marianne Dreams* was made into an exciting TV serial, which you may have seen. She has also written several books about a girl called Polly and a wolf who is always trying to eat her. 'The Spell' is one of these stories.

The Spell

CATHERINE STORR

The wolf shut his large book with a loud bang.

'Of course! What I need is a spell! A spell which would make that stupid Polly come to see me, asking me to be kind enough to eat her up,' he said.

He was amazed that the idea hadn't occurred to him before. In the book he had just been reading there was no shortage of spells. Beautiful princesses got turned into frogs, frogs turned into handsome princes; kings were trapped and enchanted by witches, several small juicy children were forced, by magic, to work for giants and ogres or other unpleasant characters and were often in the gravest danger of being eaten. If all this could happen to princesses and princes, why shouldn't a perfectly ordinary little Polly be made, by a spell, to come and look for a very respectable wolf? And evenmade to ask him to eat her? Without any fuss, and without any of this endless argument. The wolf was bored with argument. All he wanted was a good meal, and to know that at last he had got the better of Polly, clever as she was supposed to be.

He thought carefully. He had to find a really reliable spell. He didn't want one which was going to run out at an awkward moment. Or one which never got going. The wolf put some money into a small leather bag which he tied securely round his neck, and trotted off to see what the High Street shops had to offer.

A shop window piled with saucepans, pails, baskets, cat litter and bottles of different-coloured mixtures first attracted him. A solid-looking stool was labelled 'Built to last'. This sounded promising. The wolf didn't want a long-lasting stool, of course, but if this shop sold reliable stools, why not sure-fire spells? He was encouraged by seeing that a bottle of purplish liquid was apparently called MAGI-CLEAN. He went boldly into the shop.

'I want a spell,' the wolf said to a stupid-looking girl who was leaning against a white cupboard and reading a newspaper.

'A what?'

'A spell.'

'Don't keep them. No one asks for them nowadays,' the girl said, without taking her eyes from the page in front of her.

'Yes you do. I saw one in the window.'

'Must have been a mistake. Told you, we don't keep them. They're out of date,' the girl said, still not looking at the wolf.

'I tell you, I saw it. Here. Look!' the wolf said, seeing more bottles of the same purplish stuff on a shelf near by.

'What, that? Why didn't you say so?' the girl said. She snatched a bottle from the shelf, and began searching in a drawer for a paper bag.

'That'll be seventy-nine pence,' she said.

'Wait a moment. What does it do?' the wolf asked.

'What do you mean, what does it do?'

'What I say. What does the magic do? It might not be what I need. What I want is a simple spell which will make a small girl . . .'

'I don't know what you're on about. Can't you read? This is for cleaning out ovens. Says so on the label,' the girl said.

She put the bottle within an inch or two of the wolf's nose. The printing on the label was very small and the wolf was unable to read a word.

'Is that all? Just cleans ovens? Nothing else?' he said, disappointed.

'What d'you expect for seventy-nine pence? A beauty cream? Though it would take more than that to make you fit to look at,' the girl said unpleasantly. She put the bottle back on its shelf and returned to her newspaper. The wolf, insulted, went quickly out of the shop.

'What a very disagreeable girl. And stupid! Even stupider than Polly,' he thought. He stopped in front of another shop window to examine his own reflection.

'I don't know what she can have meant by that remark about beauty cream. I am a remarkably good-looking wolf,' he decided, and, slightly comforted by what he had seen, went on his way.

He stopped next to visit a food store. He found it difficult to pass by the containers of frozen meat, though he knew from past experience that you had to wait for hours before you could get your teeth properly into those tempting-looking hunks. He passed the shelves of bread and biscuits. At last he found what he was looking for. A small packet. On the outside was printed 'TENDERISER. FOR ANY KIND OF MEAT.'

He carried three packets to the check-out desk.

'Does it really work?' he asked the girl who rang up the cost on the cash register.

'Like magic,' she said.

'Have you got any more magic spells?' the wolf asked, interested. But by this time the girl

was attending to the customer behind the wolf, and she took no notice of his question, only pushed his three packets of tenderiser towards him.

Outside the shop, the wolf looked carefully at the instructions on the packet. 'SPRINKLE A FEW DROPS ON THE MEAT BEFORE COOKING. LEAVE FOR TEN TO FIFTEEN MINUTES BEFORE PUTTING IN THE OVEN,' he read. He opened the packet. Inside was a small bottle.

Very carefully the wolf sprinkled three or four drops on to his own front leg. 'If it makes me tender, it really is magic,' he thought.

He stood still on the pavement, watching the clock on the clock tower. At the end of ten minutes, he opened his mouth and brought his front leg towards it.

'Wow! That hurt!' he said in surprise as his teeth met his own skin. He looked quickly round. He would not have liked Polly to see him testing his own tenderness in this way. She might have thought it was stu . . . not a very clever thing to do.

He continued to walk down the street, looking in all the windows as he went. Presently he stopped outside a shop called simply HEALTH. In the window were two pictures. One was of a miserable-looking woman with a great many wrinkles, bags under her eyes and hair like string. The other showed the same woman, but this time, with a smooth skin and shining hair. In her hand she held a box of globules to which she was pointing. Under the picture were the words, 'Magical transformation. I grew ten years younger in a single night.'

'That is something like magic!' the wolf thought admiringly, and he pushed open the shop door and went straight in.

'I see you have boxes of magic pills. What I want is a spell . . .' he began saying to the anxious-looking woman behind the counter.

'A smell? Ah, yes. Can I suggest these charming lavender bags . . . so delicious. You can just sprinkle them about your linen cupboard . . .' she began.

'No, you don't understand. I want a magic potion. Something you drink. Or eat. I'll have a couple of those boxes of globules the lady in the window has in her hand,' the wolf said. Making Polly younger when he caught her would also make her tenderer and possibly stupider. While the worried woman was finding the pills, the wolf wandered round the shop. The more he looked, the more sure he became that this was the right place for spells. So many bottles full of different coloured fluids! So many small packages done up with gold string, with pictures of herbs outside. When the wolf caught sight of a black cat stalking through the shop, and then saw an old-fashioned twig broom leaning in a corner, he knew he had at last found a witch's lair.

'That's her broom, I suppose,' he said to the worried woman.

'The besom, yes. We like the old customs here,' she said, making a neat parcel out of the two boxes of pills.

'Do you use it too? I suppose it's strong enough,' the wolf said. The woman looked as if she'd be quite a load.

'I find it far better than any of the modern brooms,' the woman said. 'Can I interest you in anything else?' she asked.

'I'd be very much interested in anything that could make a young girl behave kindly to wol . . . to animals,' the wolf said.

'Do you mean she isn't kind to our dumb friends?' the woman asked, shocked.

'She certainly isn't.'

'Treats them badly? Pulls the wings off flies? Doesn't look after her pets?'

'Starves them,' the wolf said sadly.

'But that's terrible!'

'Haven't you got something which would change her? A bottle of medicine? Some more pills?'

The anxious woman shook her head. 'Nothing will change a bad nature like that except education. Someone must take her in hand

and teach her. What a terrible story! Perhaps you could give her little lessons and tell her how wickedly she's behaving?'

'I've been trying for years. But it's a very difficult case,' the wolf said sadly. He picked up his parcel and left the shop.

A day or two later, Polly was upstairs in her bedroom when she heard a loud knock on the front door. She thought of going down to see who it was, but she had learned to be careful so

she opened the window and looked cautiously out to see who was below. There was nothing and no one to be seen.

She went downstairs and saw a small parcel lying on the doormat inside the front door. A label tied on it said simply 'TO POLLY.'

'A present. But it isn't my birthday,' Polly thought. She sat down on the mat and tore off the paper.

Inside was a round pill-box. The piece of paper stuck to the lid had writing on it, which read:

MAGIC!
UNTIL YOU TRY THIS MAGIC REMEDY YOU WILL NEVER BELIEVE HOW THE WRINKLES FADE AWAY – THE SKIN BECOMES CLEAR AND YOUTHFUL
YOUR STEP REGAINS ITS SPRING
LIFE LOOKS PROMISING
MAKES YOU TEN YEARS YOUNGER.
TAKE THREE GLOBULES AFTER EACH MEAL

The pill-box was full of large green globules.

As Polly was looking at them, she heard the letter-box rattle and the end of a long black nose pushed itself a short way through.

'Am oom om em?' a muffled voice asked.

'I don't understand,' Polly said.

'Bother. Can't talk with that trap thing round my mouth. I said, Have you got them?' the wolf's ordinary voice said from the other side of the door.

'The green globules?' Polly asked.

'From a friend,' said the voice.

'What am I supposed to do with them?'

'Swallow them, of course. How can anyone be quite so stupid?' the voice said, impatient.

'But it says on the box that they will take away my wrinkles, and I haven't got any,' Polly said.

'Perhaps the globules will prevent your getting any.'

'And they are supposed to make my skin clear and my step springy.'

'Well? You don't want to have muddy skin and to plod around like a camel, do you?' the wolf asked.

'And, Wolf! It says the globules will make me ten years younger,' Polly called out.

'And that much tenderer. A delicate morsel. Like one of those very small sucking pigs you see sometimes in butchers' shops. A very small Polly . . .' The wolf's voice died away into happy dreams of guzzling greed.

'But . . .'

'Don't let's have any of this endless talk, girl. Eat up your nice globules and don't argue,' the wolf said.

'But, Wolf, you haven't counted. The globules will make me ten years younger.'

'Hurry up and swallow them, then. I'm hungry.'

'Wolf, I am seven years old,' Polly said.

'Seven. Eight. Six. What does it matter now?'

'You aren't very good at numbers, Wolf. I am seven. If I eat these globules, and they make me ten years younger, how old do you think I shall be?'

'Two? One and a half? Six months? All good ages. Delicious ages. Just what I enjoy most,' the wolf said.

'You can't count, Wolf. If you take ten away from seven, it leaves minus three.'

'What is minus?' the wolf's voice asked suspiciously.

'It would mean that I wouldn't get born for another three years.'

'Say that again. Slowly,' the voice said.

'If... I... eat... these globules and they make me... ten... years... younger... I shan't get born again as a baby for another... three... years.'

There was a short silence.

'Are you sure of that?' the voice asked.

'Numbers is my best subject at school,' Polly said.

'Another three years, you said. You mean that there wouldn't be any Polly for that long?

I'd have to wait for three whole years?'

'That's right,' Polly said.

'And then you would get born? A small, fat, juicy Polly? Who wouldn't have learned to talk? No, it's no good. I can't wait that long,' the wolf's voice said from the other side of the door. Polly heard a disappointed groan.

'Do you want me to start straight away?' Polly called out. There was no answer. Polly peeped through the letter-box and saw a dejected-looking tail disappearing towards the garden gate.

A second box of green globules flew off to one side of the owner of the tail. On the other side went a small bottle of tenderiser. 'Spells. You can't trust them now like you could in the good old days,' the wolf muttered angrily as, once more disappointed, he trotted towards his own home.

* * *

What can I say about COLIN WEST? He obviously has a great sense of humour. He went to college to learn how to illustrate books but then discovered that he could make up funny rhymes as well. He wrote the next three verses, and you'll find plenty more poems to make you smile in his book called *Not To Be Taken Seriously*.

Jocelyn, My Dragon

COLIN WEST

My dragon's name is Jocelyn,
He's something of a joke.
For Jocelyn is very tame,
He doesn't like to maul or maim,
Or breathe a fearsome fiery flame;
He's much too smart to smoke.

And when I take him to the park
The children form a queue,
And say, 'What lovely eyes of red!'
As one by one they pat his head.
And Jocelyn is so well-bred,
He only eats a few!

Samantha

COLIN WEST

In the jungle skipped Samantha,
For her troubles to forget,
When she met a hungry panther
Who'd not had his breakfast yet.

But Samantha had some flowers,
So she gave the beast the bunch.
They became good friends for hours –
Then he ate her up for lunch.

Geraldine Giraffe

COLIN WEST

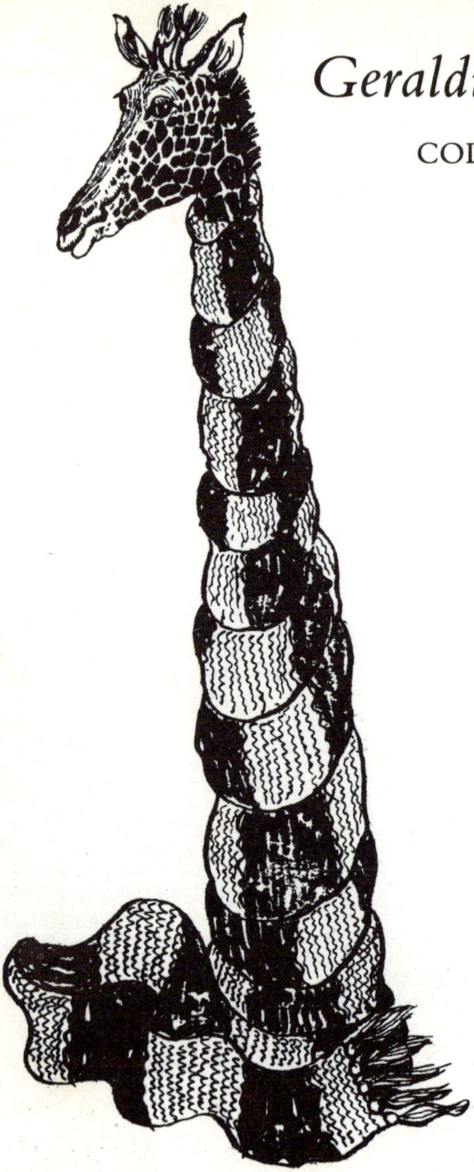

The
longest
ever
woolly
scarf
was
worn
by
Geraldine
Giraffe.
Around
her
neck
the
scarf
she
wound,
but
still
it
trailed
upon
the
ground.

'The Windlecombe Witch' is *told* by one of the children in the story; it is *written* by ANTONIA BARBER, who is my sister. A few years ago she wrote a ghost story which was made into an exciting film called 'The Amazing Mr Blunden'. Antonia lives in an oast house in Kent with her three children, Jonathan, Nicholas and Gemma. They also have one dog, three cats and lots of chickens.

The Windlecombe Witch

ANTONIA BARBER

We were in the village shop one morning when we first saw the witch. We had gone down to buy some sweets and Mrs Barton greeted us warmly from behind the counter, delighted at the chance to show off her knowledge of the newcomers.

'Here be the new schoolmaster's children, then,' she said informatively to the mothers and small children who crowded the tiny store.

Everyone stared at us with interest. Tom and I smiled politely, but Robbie put his thumb in his mouth and stared crossly back at them. A stout, friendly woman bent down to speak to him.

'So you've come all the way from London to live in Windlecombe,' she said encouragingly. 'How do you like the country, then?'

Robbie glared at her, unsmiling. 'I don't,' he said.

She was taken aback. 'You don't like it, my dear! Why ever not?'

Robbie sighed. 'I miss my Granny,' he said gloomily.

The women smiled at each other sympathetically, relieved that there was nothing personal in Robbie's dislike.

'She used to live very near to us in London,' I explained. 'Robbie is very fond of her.'

I could have added that Robbie was Granny's pet, and that he had run to her whenever anyone grumbled at him and that he had been a perfect misery ever since we moved away. But I didn't because after all, he is my brother, and you can't tell tales about your brother to someone you've just met.

'You'll all be going to your Daddy's school, then?' put in another woman inquiringly.

Tom looked offended. '*I'm* much too old for the village school!' he told her. '*I* shall go to school in Torton, but Alice will be there for a year, and Robbie is starting next term.'

They nodded and chuckled approvingly. 'Ee's a big boy, then, i'n 'ee?' said one woman, but Robbie was not to be moved by flattery.

'You come in for some sweeties, then?' asked Mrs Barton. 'You go ahead, my dears. Never mind these ladies, they'm just gossiping.'

We chose from among the bright jars and she put the sweets into twisted cones of paper. Then, just as she was handing us our change, the bell clanked on the shop door and a gust of wind blew around us.

We turned to see an old lady in black, with quite the ugliest face I'd ever seen. She was bent over a stick, and she looked just like the witches in story-books. She had a strange effect on everyone in the shop. The chatter seemed to die away; the toddlers hid behind their mothers' skirts; and even Mrs Barton's fat old

dog bristled slightly, and backed up behind the counter.

'Ello, then, Miss Tulliver,' said Mrs Barton, squeezing her way round to the post-office part of the shop. 'You come in for your pension, dear?'

We watched, fascinated, as the old lady received the money and then made a few purchases; some salt, a reel of cotton, a packet of pins. Then she turned and hobbled out, and the door clanked shut behind her.

The toddlers came out of hiding; the fat dog rushed forward and barked from behind the safety of the glass door.

Robbie was staring after her. Suddenly he turned and his face shone with excitement. 'Gosh!' he said, 'was that a real witch?'

Mrs Barton laughed. 'Why, that was old Miss Tulliver,' she said. 'She isn't no witch! I'm sure she's a right good soul at heart!'

But Robbie was not convinced. He stuck a sweet in his mouth and looked very thoughtful.

'Of course, she *is* a witch,' he said when we got outside. 'I could tell soon as I saw her!'

'She's a witch all right!' said a voice behind us, and we turned to see a fat freckled boy sitting on the bench outside the shop. 'Anyone knows that,' he went on. 'She lives down there in the wood.'

He pointed to a path through the trees, along

which the little black figure could be seen hobbling.

Tom looked very superior. 'Nonsense!' he said. 'She can't possibly be. There are no such things as witches!'

The fat boy snorted. 'There are too!' he said. 'What d'you know about witches? Come down here from London! You'm just never seen a witch before!'

'How do you know she's a witch?' I asked, half inclined to believe him.

'Stands to reason,' he said. 'What's she do all day long? I'll tell you. She makes little dolls as looks like people, an' she sticks pins in 'em. That's magic! If she sticks pins in the doll's leg, someone gets a pain in their leg, an' if she sticks a pin in its back, they get a pain in the back. I shouted after 'er once, and next day I got a tummy-ache. I bet she made a doll like me and stuck a pin in its tummy!'

Tom snorted disbelievingly.

'How do you know she makes dolls?' I asked, remembering uneasily that she had bought a reel of cotton and a packet of pins.

'Folks 'ave seen 'em. 'Er little house is full of 'em!'

'Well, I've never heard such rubbish!' said Tom with all the scorn of a townsman for country superstitions.

'All right,' said the boy crossly, 'if she i'nt a

witch, you go down an' look in 'er window: see if you don't see them dolls hanging there, all stuck full of pins!'

Tom didn't look keen, but he repeated stubbornly, 'Of course she's not a witch.'

'I bet you're scared, though!' said the boy.

'We're not scared at all,' I told him, 'and Tom's quite right: there are no witches; our father said so. We just don't want to go looking in people's windows that's all.'

The boy smiled slyly. 'I'll tell all the other kids the townies are scared,' he threatened.

Robbie had been silent all this time. Now he said suddenly: 'Well, I'm not scared, and I want to see the witch and the dolls!' And away he ran. By the time we had recovered from our surprise, he was fast disappearing among the trees.

'We'd better go after him,' said Tom.

The fat boy cackled and his voice followed us as we ran: 'You mind the witch don't get you!'

At first the wood was leafy green, bright with sunlight and noisy with birds. But as we went farther in, the sun passed behind a cloud, and it seemed cold and gloomy. We caught glimpses of Robbie's red jumper flitting ahead of us along the path. Once, when we had nearly caught up with him, I tripped over a tree root, and by the time Tom had helped me up and wiped the blood from my scratched knee, Robbie had gone again.

We followed him deeper into the darkening wood, and I began to be afraid. The fat boy's jeering voice echoed in my ears, and I took hold of Tom's hand, pretending that it was only in case I tripped again.

Then we saw light gleaming ahead and came out into a clearing where the wood ran beside a meadow, and there was a house, a pretty house and yet with a strange air about it.

Robbie was standing in the open doorway, and Tom and I paused at the edge of the trees, half expecting that the witch would drag him inside and that we should have the fearful job of rescuing him!

But Robbie turned and called, 'There's no one here; the witch must be out. But the dolls are here and they *have* got pins sticking in them!'

My heart sank. The boy had been right and our father was wrong. Like us he was a townsman and knew nothing about the mysteries in the deep woods. There *were* such things as witches!

'Come and look,' called Robbie gaily, but I was much too scared.

'Come away,' I told him, 'we have to go.'

'I won't!' he said, stamping his foot. 'Not until you've seen them.'

'We'll have to humour him,' said Tom, 'you know how stubborn he is. Let's hope she's nowhere about.'

We tiptoed nervously across to the door of the cottage and looked in. The dolls were everywhere, on shelves and on the window-sills, with pins in their arms and legs.

I felt quite cold. 'Gosh,' I said, 'there must be an awful lot of people she doesn't like! Do you think they are all getting pains?'

I had a horrible thought. If she caught us, would she make dolls like us and stick pins in them? I had once had earache and I certainly didn't want that again.

Then, as we gazed with thumping hearts, we heard a sound behind us and turning we saw the witch herself, standing a few yards away.

I was very frightened: she seemed even uglier and stranger than she had in the little shop.

For a long time we just stared at each other; then she asked, 'Did you want something, you children?'

We didn't know what to say. We couldn't very well say, 'We came to find out if you were a witch, and now we find that you are.'

In desperation I stammered, 'We . . . came to see the dolls. They're awfully nice. Do . . . do you make them?'

She went on staring at us for what seemed an age, and then, surprisingly, she smiled, and she wasn't nearly so frightening.

'I do make them,' she said, coming closer. 'Would you like to see some?' The voice which had sounded so quavery in the shop, now sounded quiet, almost friendly.

We nodded, and she led the way into the house.

'I'll show you some I've finished,' she said, 'not these old things. They haven't had their arms and legs sewn on yet, they're just pinned together.'

She went across to a large chest, and lifting the lid, she took out the prettiest rag-doll I'd ever seen. It was dressed in blue gingham and had a little sunbonnet framing a smiling face.

'Oh, how lovely!' I exclaimed, quite forgetting in my surprise that I was talking to a witch. 'Did you really make it all by yourself?'

'Indeed, I did,' she said and fetched out another, a soldier doll in a bright red jacket.

Robbie reached out his hands in delight. 'Can I hold it?' he asked.

The witch handed it to him, and her dark eyes seemed to shine in her ugly face at the sight of his pleasure.

It was hard to believe that they could do people harm, but why would an old lady have so many dolls if not for magic?

The same thought was troubling Tom for he asked abruptly, 'Why do you make so many?'

I guessed that it had taken all his courage to ask, but, of course, he had to have some explanation with which to face the fat boy.

'Why, I make them for children in hospitals,' explained the old lady. 'A rag-doll is a comfy thing to have when you're in bed with a pain. They cheer the little ones up and make them get better faster.' She looked rather sad as she went on, 'I'm very fond of children, but I never had a family myself. And the children in the village, well, I think they're afraid of me, poor dears. It's my ugly old face, you know, but then, a face is something it's hard to change. I used to try to talk to them once, but, like as not, they'd burst into tears, so I thought it kinder to leave them alone. So I make my little dolls and I send them to the children in hospitals, and when they like my dolls, it's as if they liked me.'

Robbie seized her hand. '*I* like you!' he said eagerly. 'I really do! I think you're an absolutely super witch!'

Tom and I were horrified, and the old lady looked surprised and hurt.

'A witch, my dear!' she exclaimed. 'Is that what they told you? Do *you* think I'm a witch?'

'Of course you are!' said Robbie happily. 'Stands to reason! You live in the woods and you make dolls for children who have a pain. If they've got a pain in their leg,' he explained, 'you stick a pin in the doll's leg and the pain goes away. That's magic!'

The old lady smiled. 'Well,' she said, 'I never

thought of it quite like that. I suppose I do in a way. Does that make me a witch?'

He eyed the red-coated soldier with longing. 'I've got a sort of pain in my foot,' he said. 'Would you like to stick a pin in that soldier doll and give it to me?'

'Robbie!' I said, very shocked, 'you haven't got a bad foot and you know Mummy says you must never ask for things!'

He scowled. 'I might get a pain; then I could have the doll all ready.'

I didn't know what to say; I was so embarrassed.

But the witch didn't seem to mind. 'I don't know if it would stop any pains,' she said, 'but if it makes you happy, you can have the little soldier and welcome.'

Robbie looked at Tom and me with our disapproving faces and then, clutching the doll, he sidled closer to the witch. 'Thank you very much,' he said in his best party manner. He smiled up at her and went on, 'You can be one of my grannies, if you like. It would be very handy for me to have a granny who was a witch.'

'Why, I can't think of anything I should like better!' said the witch, and so it was agreed between them.

As we made our way through the woods, with Robbie clutching his soldier doll under one arm, he said cheerfully, 'You'll all have to be jolly careful not to grumble at me now, or I'll get my Granny Witch to put a spell on you!' And he skipped on ahead of us down the path.

Tom and I looked at each other, and then we laughed. 'Well,' he said, 'seeing what a misery Robbie's been ever since we left London, and how nice he is now, I think there must be a special pin sewn up inside that doll, to put a spell on him!'

We walked on in silence for a while, and then I asked, 'What will you say to that fat boy? Do you think she is really a witch, a good one, I mean?'

Tom looked very superior again. 'Nonsense!' he said. 'There are no such things as witches!'

Boys, I thought, they're always so sure about everything.

But I wondered . . .

* * *

Acknowledgements

The author and publishers gratefully acknowledge permission to reprint copyright material to the following:

'The Chancellor Who Wouldn't Smile' copyright © Pamela Oldfield from *The Terribly Plain Princess,* first published by Brockhampton Press (now Hodder & Stoughton Children's Books) in hardback, and also published under the title of 'The Chancellor Who Wouldn't Smile' by Beaver Books (a division of the Hutchinson Publishing Group) in paperback. 'Buster's Day Out' copyright © Pamela Oldfield from *The Gumby Gang On Holiday,* first published by Blackie & Son Ltd. The Literary Trustees of Walter de la Mare and the Society of Authors as their representatives for 'The Ride-By-Nights' and 'Chicken'. Faber & Faber Ltd for 'The Wind in a Frolic' and 'The Rainbow' from *Mustard, Pepper and Salt* by Alison Uttley, and for 'The Spell' from *Tales of Polly and the Hungry Wolf* by Catherine Storr. Methuen Children's Books for 'Bad Sir Brian Botany' from *When We Were Very Young* by A. A. Milne. 'A Puffin Called Percy' from *Bobby Brewster's Kite* and 'Penny for the Guy' from *Bobby Brewster's Bee*, both copyright © H. E. Todd 1967 and 1972, first published by Brockhampton Press (now Hodder & Stoughton Children's Books). Penguin Books Ltd for 'Catnap', 'Oh Erica, Not Again!' and 'Who's Scared Now?' copyright © 1980 by Max Fatchen from *Songs For my Dog and Other People* (Puffin Books 1982) pp. 10, 49 and 28, and 'Babbling and Gabbling' and 'It's Winter, It's Winter' by Kit Wright from *Hot Dog and Other Poems* (Kestrel Books 1981) pp. 47 and 71, text copyright © 1981 Kit Wright. Hutchinson Publishing Group Ltd for 'Jocelyn My Dragon', 'Samantha' and 'Geraldine Giraffe' from *Not To Be Taken Seriously* by Colin West. 'The Windlecombe Witch' copyright © Antonia Barber, originally published in *Winter Tales for Children* (2) by Macmillan Children's Books.

The publishers have made every effort to trace copyright holders. If we have inadvertently omitted to acknowledge anyone we should be most grateful if this would be brought to our attention for correction at the first opportunity.